W9-AKE-005

OCT 3 1 2014

DATE DUE

AUG 2 6 2016			
			PRINTED IN U.S.A.

FEB 0 5 2014

TIME-LIFE
Early Learning Program

Purple Parrots
eating
Carrots

TIME
LIFE for
Children ™

ALEXANDRIA, VIRGINIA

Note to Parents

Purple Parrots Eating Carrots is a collection of original stories and poems that enables even the youngest child to experience the joy of independent reading. Throughout the book, rebus pictures take the place of certain words. Move your finger beneath the words as you read each story aloud to your child. When you come to a rebus picture, point to it and have your child "read" that image. By following your finger as you read, she will begin to understand that printed words are read from left to right and from top to bottom, and that they represent spoken language.

The book contains both simple and complex rebus pictures. In the story "Fair Play and Fowl," for example, some rebus pictures stand for not only individual words, but for different syllables within the same word. This is intended to help your child discover that sounds work together to form words.

Once your child realizes that he can take part in reading a rebus story, encourage him to create tales of his own: Start by writing down a story your child tells you, using his drawings in place of as many words as possible, then read the story aloud together. After a few such readings, turn the tables and watch your child delight in "reading" the story to you.

Come along with me and discover how words and pictures can tell a story together!

Calling all  and and !

Would you like to act as words?

You in a rebus—it's all the rage!

For a reading adventure, just turn the .

Table of Contents

Clever from Head to Toe

I'm a very clever fellow.

Look at all that I can do:

I can wink one  .

I can lace up my  .

I can wiggle my

and crinkle my .

I can stand on my

and count all my .

I can hop on one 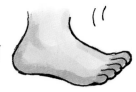 .

I can pucker my  .

I can balance an

on two fingertips.

I can do so many things,

though I've only named a few.

And if you ask me nicely,

I'll show them all to you.

7

Numbers, Numbers Everywhere

One day when Bunny was washing his numbers

And hanging them out to dry,

A wind sprang up that whistled and roared

And blew them into the sky.

Numbers, numbers in the air,

Numbers, numbers everywhere!

The numbers sailed both far and wide—

They landed all over the countryside:

The  **1** fell into the 🪣.

The **2** came down in a 👟.

The **3** got stuck in a honey 🐝,

And the **4** was split in two.

The **5** and the **6**

slid under some 🧱;

The **7** crashed onto the ground.

The **8** and the **9** clung fast to the line,

But the **10** was never found.

Bird's Secret Hiding Place

One day Duck and Bear and Squirrel and Bird were

playing hide-and-seek. was "it." He covered

his  and began counting to **10**.

1, 2, 3, 4, 5...

 scampered up a nearby  while

hid behind a tall garden 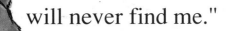 .

said, "I am going to hide in a secret

place where will never find me."

"...6, 7, 8, 9, 10," said . "Ready or not,

here I come!"

 opened his 👁 👁 and looked around.

There was no one in sight. But it was not long before

poked his head around the to see

what was going on. spotted him and cried,

"I see you, !"

Just then found a large and

cracked it open.

heard the noise overhead. He looked up and

saw hiding in the . "I see you,

!" shouted .

"Now all I have to do is find ,"

said , "and I will win the game! I'm the

world's best hide-and-seek player!"

looked in every single place he could

think of, but was nowhere to be found.

and   laughed. "   is

hiding in a secret place," they said. "We'll give you a hint:

We can see her but you cannot."

was thoroughly puzzled. "Perhaps I am

not the world's best hide-and-seek player after all," he

thought to himself.

Finally  exclaimed, " I give up! I can't

find you,  ."

"Here I am!" said  . "I am right above you.

I am sitting in your  ."

"What a clever friend you are," said  .

And he smiled from  to  .

Kitty's Purr-fect Picture

Pretty Kitty, bright and witty

drew a picture of the city.

She started with a △ .

Then she drew a ▢ .

Then she drew three

◯ ◯ ◯ :

One here,

one here,

one there.

Next she drew two ◯◯ .

Then she added lots

of 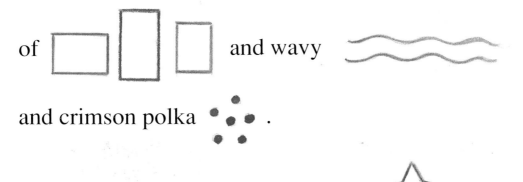 and wavy

and crimson polka . .

To finish up her picture, Kitty drew a .

Then proudly told her city, "How beautiful you are!"

"That's a picture-
purr-fect city, kitty!"

19

The Land of Let's Pretend

I'm going on a journey
To the land of "Let's Pretend."
Would you like to go there, too?
It's just around the bend.
I shut my eyes and soon I see
A whole new world ahead of me:

Polar  in rocking

Turtles baking

Kangaroos in tennis

And lions with bow

21

Persian

in cowboy

sailing

22

Dancing

in powdered

And wearing

Baby  knitting

flying

24

Twin with bright

And riding

Purple _____ eating

Elephants on

Nimble foxes carrying

And peacocks sewing

Now I have to say good-bye;
Our journey's at an end.
I hope to see you soon once more
In the land of "Let's Pretend."

Gee, those carrots were delicious! If you went to a magic land, what would you eat there?

Molly McNair's Trip to the Fair

Here's your chance to create your own rebus story! When you come to each group of three pictures, choose any one picture to complete the rhyme. See how many different stories you can make!

This is the story of Molly McNair
Who went to the fair to buy a

She met a lad who stopped to chat.
Said he, "I'm here to buy a

She met a maiden dressed in green
Who came to buy a

She met a prince with wobbly knees.
He was there in search of

She met a fisherman, hearty and hale
Who sailed to town to buy a

She met a farmer holding a note
That said, "Be sure to buy a

It was quite a day for Molly McNair
Who plumb forgot to buy that

The High-Flying Monster

One day Duck and Bear and Squirrel and Bird were

walking in the  . Suddenly they

heard something flying overhead. They looked up to see

what it was.

"It's a FLYING MONSTER!" exclaimed  .

"Look at those ugly yellow ," said  .

"Look at those big pointed ," said  .

"Look at that long, spiked tail," said  .

33

"Let's hide!" said . "The 🙂 is coming

right toward us!"

The animals ran behind a big and

huddled close together.

 poked his head out from behind the big

to see if the was following them. "Be careful," said

. "Don't take any chances."

"Shhh, not so loud," said . "The will

hear us."

Just then a  and a ran into the clearing.

"Here it is," said the .

" We're lucky," said the . "Our kite isn't even torn."

"A kite!" cried . "Our  is a kite!"

 smiled broadly. "I knew it all the time," she said.

"I wasn't even scared," said . "I never get scared."

"I never get scared, either," said .

Suddenly there was a loud "CRASH!" behind them.

"This time it's really a monster!" yelled .

"Make a run for it," said and .

just smiled.

"There's no need to hide," she said. "This monster is only a runaway ."

Then looked at her friends crouched behind the . "Are you *sure* you never get scared?" she asked.

and and grinned.

"Well, maybe sometimes," they laughed. "But just a little!"

Turtle in the Rain

The [turtle] manages very well

Inside his warm and cozy [shell].

Drops of [rain] don't bother him;

He's got an [umbrella] built right in.

Fair Play and Fowl

One day a  was walking through the

when he met a . The said:

I am happy **2 C** you.

You see, am hungry and **U**

will be a tasty meal **4** me.

"But I am quite thin," said the . "There is a

fatter coming down the

behind me. She will be a much tastier meal for you."

Then the  added:

If U 🥫 wait 4 a while,

you would 🐝 very wise, indeed.

"Perhaps you are right," said the . So he

let the go on her way.

The waited. Sure enough, a fatter

soon came down the .

The  said:

👁 am happy 2 **C** **U**.

You see, 👁 am very hungry and **U** will 🐝 a tasty meal **4** me.

42

"But I am quite thin," said the .

"There is a much fatter  coming down

the  behind me. She will be a much tastier

meal for you." Then the  added:

If U  w+ 8 4

a while, U would

very w+ 👁 👁 indeed.

"Perhaps you are right," said the .

So he let that  go on her way too.

The  waited. Sure enough, he soon heard some-

one coming down the . But that someone was not a

fat . It was a huge, brown .

The said:

👁 M happy **2 C U**.

U C, 👁 M very hungry and **U**

will 🐝 a tasty m+ 🪱 **4** me.

When the  heard these words, he ran

as fast as he could out of the , and

he was never seen again.

Won't You Come In, Pete Pigley?
A tongue-twisting pig tale

Do I have to come inside already, Papa?

It's past playtime, Pete. Please pick up your toys.

I just want to bounce my once more and play with the other boys.

The will soon be setting, son. In seconds it will be dark.

But Pop, I have to find my . I think they're in the park!

47

I picked some purple-petaled posies—they're a present just for you!

Cowboy Cat's Nap

There once was a silly old

who constantly wore a black .

It's even been said

that he wore it to .

Now imagine a doing that!

The Saga of Johnny McKay

In this story about Johnny McKay, *you* get to decide what happens. When you come to each group of three pictures, choose one picture to complete the rhyme. Johnny McKay likes to travel, so make up as many adventures as you can!

This is the tale of Johnny McKay
Who went on a trip and lost his way.
He started out in Idaho
While searching for a

From there he traveled to New York
To see if he could find a

Next he flew a plane to Maine
And tried in vain to find a

His plane was grounded in a fog,
So he went looking for a

Then on he trekked to Yellowstone
To find the world's best

But all he found was a cardboard box
Filled with socks and rocks and

And that ends the tale of Johnny McKay,
For on that day he lost his way.
Just where he is, we do not know—
Perhaps he's back in Idaho!

Picture-a-Word

Can you put the pictures together in each box to make one word? To check your answer, follow the blue line until you reach a picture.

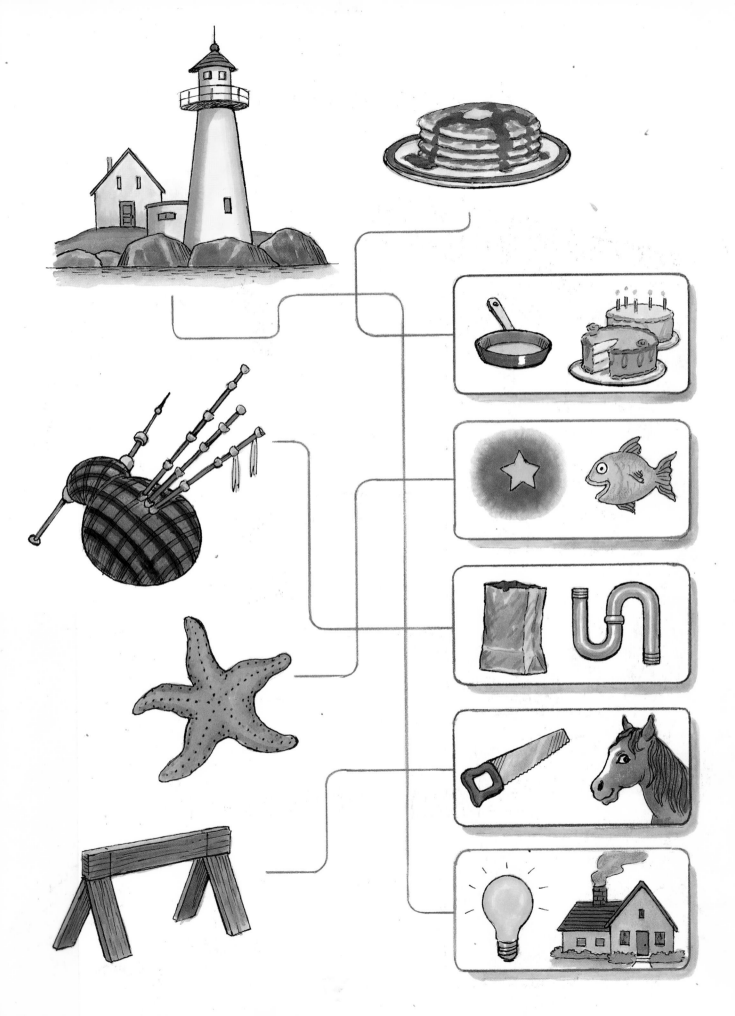

Pete Pigley's Monkey Mischief
A bedtime pig tale

Jungle Walk

"Small!" exclaimed the . "I never thought

of myself as +ing small."

Now the  was  very happy and he

walked sadly through the  until he

a . The  said:

M+, how big
and tall **U R** !

"Thank **U**," said the . Then he added:

But how sad **4 U**
2  so small.

"Small!" exclaimed the  . "I never thought

of m+ 👁 +self as 🐝 +ing small."

🏚 now the 🐒 was 🪢 very happy. He

walked sadly through the 🌴 until he 🪚 a

🦜 . The 🦜 said:

M+ 👁 , how big and
t+ 🔩 U R!

"Thank U ," said the 🐒 . Then he added:

But how sad 4 U
2 🐝 so sm+ 🔩 .

62

"SMALL!" exclaimed the  . " What makes

U th+ INK that 👁 M small? 🐜 and specks of

dust R small, but I'm 🪨 small at all." Then he added:

The size 👁 M I'm

con+ ⛺ 2 🐝 ,

4 I'm the perfect

s+ 👁 👁 4 me.

Then the 🦜 waved fare+ 🏚 and flew

happily on his way.

TIME-LIFE for CHILDREN™

Publisher: Robert H. Smith
Managing Editor: Neil Kagan
Editorial Directors: Jean Burke Crawford,
   Patricia Daniels, Allan Fallow, Karin Kinney
Editorial Coordinator: Elizabeth Ward
Product Managers: Cassandra Ford, Margaret Mooney
Assistant Product Manager: Shelley L. Schimkus
Production Manager: Prudence G. Harris
Administrative Assistant: Rebecca C. Christoffersen
Editorial Consultant: Sara Mark
Special Contributor: Jacqueline A. Ball

Produced by Joshua Morris Publishing, Inc.
Wilton, Connecticut 06897.
Series Director: Michael J. Morris
Creative Director: William N. Derraugh
Illustrator: Margaret Sanfilipo
Author: Burton Marks
Design Consultant: Francis G. Morgan
Designers: Marty Heinritz, Nora Voutas

CONSULTANTS

Dr. Lewis P. Lipsitt, an internationally recognized specialist on childhood development, was the 1990 recipient of the Nicholas Hobbs Award for science in the service of children. He serves as science director for the American Psychological Association and is a professor of psychology and medical science at Brown University, where he is director of the Child Study Center.

Dr. Judith A. Schickedanz, an authority on the education of preschool children, is an associate professor of early childhood education at the Boston University School of Education, where she also directs the Early Childhood Learning Laboratory. Her published work includes *More Than the ABC's: Early Stages of Reading and Writing Development* as well as several textbooks and many scholarly papers.

First printing. Printed in Hong Kong.
Published simultaneously in Canada.

Time Life Inc. is a wholly owned subsidiary of THE TIME INC. BOOK COMPANY.

TIME-LIFE is a trademark of Time Warner Inc. U.S.A.

Time Life Inc. offers a wide range of fine publications, including home video products. For subscription information, call 1-800-621-7026, or write TIME-LIFE BOOKS, P.O. Box C-32068, Richmond, Virginia 23261-2068.

Library of Congress Cataloging-in-Publication Data
Purple parrots eating carrots.

   p. cm.–(Time-Life early learning program)
   Summary: A collection of stories and poems incorporating rebuses, designed to introduce an early understanding of reading.
   ISBN 0-8094-9262-8.—ISBN 0-8094-9263-6 (lib. bdg.)
   1. Children's literature. [1. Literature—Collections. 2. Rebuses.] I. Series. PZ5.P7898 1991 810.8′09282–dc20
                                                    90-25449
                                                    CIP
                                                    AC